POEMS OF YOUR OWN

Also by Richard Morgan

I Am Sea Glass
A Collection of Poetic Pieces

Sea Glass People
Portraits in Words and Watercolors

Sea Glass Soul
Invisible Colors

Hebrew Lessons
Poems from my Jewish Heart

Sea Glass Windows
New Poems

My Lighthouse Key
Poetry in Words and Watercolors

Painted Poetry V
2018 Exhibit Catalogue
Editor

Third Rewrite
Selected Poems

Poems for Men
Who Don't Like Poetry

POEMS OF YOUR OWN

A Guide to Writing Personal Poetry

Richard Morgan

Copyright 2021 by Richard Morgan
All rights reserved
2nd edition 2022

ISBN - 9798570966239

Kindle/Create Space
Charleston, SC

Published by
Morgan House Press
176 Carriage Summitt Way
Hendersonville, North Carolina 28791

DEDICATION

This book is dedicated to my high school English teachers, not because they taught me English, but because they never gave up on me and my embryonic writing. They encouraged this budding author long before he was even the beginnings of a bud.

Joann B. Fogarty

Daryl L. Reed

CONTENTS

1) What Is Poetry?   22
2) Why Personal Poetry?   23
3) Not Me   27
4) Write Every Day   28
5) Words Do All the Work   29
6) The Dreadful First Draft   32
7) Rights and Rewrites   33
8) Rewrites and Twilight   35
9) Hand Write   36
10) Form Issues   37
11) Feathers for Your Duck   41
12) The Five Senses   42
13) Reveal   43
14) The Snapshot and the Caveat   46

15) The Caveat - A Keyhole   48
16) First Line   50
17) Last Line   54
18) The Title   56
19) Life Is Messy   59
20) What's In, What's Out   62
21) Reading Someone Else's Poem   63
22) Figurative Language   67
23) Grammar Grabbers   69
24) Your Poetic License   72
25) Persona   74
26) The Sound of Your Words   78
27) Repetition   82
28) To Rhyme or Not   84
29) Rhyme is About Sound   86
30) Think Evolution   89
31) The Short Poem   93

32) The Right Word or Nothing 96

33) Poetic Words and Phrases 98

34) Light and Shadow 100

35) Before You Write 102

36) The Muse of Poetry 105

37) The Poet Has Two Faces 107

38) When You Get Lost and You Will 109

39 Conclusion 113

Bibliography 114

Useful References 115

Poet Point Review 119

About the Author 127

POEMS OF YOUR OWN

POEMS OF YOUR OWN

INTRODUCTION

Who Am I?

I have taught for fifty years,
written poetry longer than that.
I will share with you all I've learned,
have no reason to hold back.
Surely, I'd bust if I tried.
Together we will erase
the mystery
of writing poetry.

My 3 Tasks

to be your DOCENT (guide),
your COACH (teacher),
and your CHAMPION (advocate)

I will encourage, escort, and assist you in your efforts to record your words and write your poetry.

POEMS OF YOUR OWN

POETRY ONE

In poetry
being different helps.
Feelings, even difficult ones,
are prizes to be described.
Since each of us is one of a kind,
our words are correspondingly unique
and matchless. Then, after a time,
we find we weren't so alone
in our feelings as we thought.
We just didn't know
we had neighbors.

POEMS OF YOUR OWN

EVEN IF

Even if you write your poetry, from your heart,
and put it away in a drawer,

Even if you write your poetry, from your heart,
and show it to close family and friends,

And even if you write your poetry, from your heart,
and show it to the entire world,

You want your poetry to find a home in the hearts
of those who will hear it.

Helping you reach this end is the goal of this guide.

POEMS OF YOUR OWN

MOTHER BIRD

The mother bird
breaks the worm
into small pieces
and feeds them
to the open mouths
of her waiting chicks
knowing the whole worm,
or too large a chunk,
would cause them
to choke.

So it is with lessons;
they must be broken
into small pieces,
digestible pieces,
understandable pieces,
to avoid choking
the sapling students
who are appealing for more
with their mouths
wide open.

POEMS OF YOUR OWN

POET POINTS 1 THROUGH 39

POET POINTS

Like a compass,
giving direction,
making suggestions,
shouting encouragement,
hoping to be horribly helpful.

POEMS OF YOUR OWN

1) <u>WHAT IS POETRY</u>? (my take)

    Poetry is the careful selection
of a limited number of words
that express a feeling, or
describe an experience,
and at its best,
gives insight into the challenge
of being human.

        Prose writers
can take 50,000 words
to express themselves,
poets get 50.

Poetry is writing
refined to its essence.
Brevity is the driver.

NOTE: Poetry is not prose with line breaks.

POEMS OF YOUR OWN

2) <u>WHY PERSONAL POETRY?</u>

> We humans thrive on words,
> words put feelings on notice,
> make them more real, and
> add clarity to our memories.

In other words, personal poetry allows you
to unpack your feelings, to expose yourself,
to reveal what's inside.

> *Words, when written,*
> *crystallize history.*

> - Francis Bacon -

Poetry, your words, can give comfort.

> *If you write it,*
> *it can right you.*

Personal poetry heals.

POEMS OF YOUR OWN

A poem can be: autobiographical or fiction
(tell a lie),
rhyme or not, *(most of today's poetry does not rhyme)*
happy or sad,

silly or profound.

BUT

A poem must be: true to the human experience,

authentic,

accessible for most,

and fish market *fresh*.

POEMS OF YOUR OWN

THE BABY MAKERS

I am a seven-layer cake.
The filling between my
layers is uneven—I tilt
to one side. My icing has
a missing spot, but overall,
I feel good about myself.

My bakers weren't perfect,
but their efforts were for my sake
and I am forever grateful
and thankful to them
for they shared their sweetness
and just a trace of baking soda.

POEMS OF YOUR OWN

BROTHER

Dear brother,
my blood and bone.

You blow your warm breath
upon my frozen cheek.

You wink at my worn-out jokes,
poke fun at my overly serious side.

You touch my shoulder when I cry,
offer me your hand when I fall down.

You bear hug me when I get frenzied,
tell me with few words when I'm wrong.

You teach me to take a punch, push through
pain, practice patience, acceptance and tolerance.

You are Mom and Dad's best gift to me. Even
now, you are with me when I feel alone at night.

POEMS OF YOUR OWN

3) <u>NOT ME</u>

For some, why they won't write a poem.

First—I can't write a poem.
It's too difficult for me.
It doesn't come naturally.
Shouldn't there be an ease to it?

*Who said it was going to be easy,
or as natural as eating ice cream?
Impatience and high expectations
work mightily against you.*

*The secret
you need to know is—
every poem begins with
a dreadful first draft.*

*You won't write
a perfect poem, but
you can begin to collect
a basket of words.*

*Be patient
and your words
will become
your poem.*

POEMS OF YOUR OWN

4) <u>WRITE EVERY DAY</u>

Try this: write something every day, even if it's just a little. It could be a line, a stanza, or most of a poem. Just get it down.

> Give it fifteen dedicated minutes.
>
> One word, one line at a time.
>
> Don't wait for understanding,
>
> or a complete picture; just write.
>
> Expand your world with your poetry.
>
>> *That said, your goal is not to write a single poem, it is to write a notebook full of poems.*
>> - after Robert Frost -

Additionally, if you are not writing, then be reading, at least a poem or two each day. Keep a book of poetry wherever you sit down to read. Reading other writers' poetry is a good part of becoming a good poet.

POEMS OF YOUR OWN

5) <u>WORDS DO ALL THE WORK</u>

>The words you write must do the work for you.
>They must stand on their own.
>Your readers only know
>what you tell them
>with your words.
>You, the poet,
>are not there
>to explain what they mean.
>Be clear, concise and complete.

Think of your poem as a suitcase. You pack it the best you can and hand it over to the reader. You are done. It is the reader who opens the suitcase.

>The poet never says,
>"These are merely words,"
>for words have overwhelming weight.
>Words can create a world.
>(think Genesis... *and God said,*
>*Let there be light.*
>*And there was light.*)

>>*Your poem is a room.*
>>*It gives the reader*
>>*a place to hang out,*
>>*no small feat.*

POEMS OF YOUR OWN

DRUMBEAT

My drum set sat in our basement
next to my mother's washing machine.
She encouraged me to drum,
"Practice is what you need." I resisted,
"Practice is so boring." What I liked to do
was wait until she put a load of wash in,
wait for her to go back upstairs, and then I'd
wail away to the rhythm of the machine.

The washer had a mechanical sound
that repeated like a metronome and
the water crashing against the tub
sounded like ocean waves. Clink-clank,
squish, squash, clink-clank, squish squash.
Then after a short while, a thud
followed by a whirling sound that cued me
to do a drumroll on my cymbals.

When the wash and spin cycles were over,
and the machine was done, I'd go crazy
and hit every drum and cymbal I had until
I was exhausted by my crescendo. My mother
never told me to stop fooling around. Maybe
she didn't hear me down in the basement.
On the other hand, she could hear me
whisper a secret to my best friend.

POEMS OF YOUR OWN

POEMS OF YOUR OWN

6) THE DREADFUL FIRST DRAFT

What's the purpose of your dreadful first draft?

Yes, most, maybe all, first drafts are dreadful.

Question: how does a baseball team get to the second game of the world series?

Answer: play in the first game.

Lesson: get the dreadful first draft of your poem down so you can get on with the second...

Perfect is terrible,
it can't have children.
   - Sylvia Plath -

POEMS OF YOUR OWN

7) <u>RIGHTS AND REWRITES</u>
and the misconception...

> write,
> rewrite,
> then rewrite again

Writing a poem is to a poet like hitting a homerun is to a star baseball player. This athlete spends hundreds of hours in the batting cage developing his smooth, successful swing. Minus the practice and he's back to the minors, if lucky.

Your first draft of your poem is like one afternoon in the batting cage. You have many more ahead of you for a smooth, resonating poem, one that works. It is a fallacy to think you can do this with a carefree, easy effort. You may have the right to think that way, but it's not true, it is a misconception. Sorry, poets fill hundreds of pages with poems and their rewrites.

> *Revision isn't the cleaning up after the party;*
> *revision is the party.*
> - William Mathews -

> Print the latest draft of your poem.
> Edit it in blue ink, not red.
> Red is so cold.
> Editing is *gentle* dissection.

POEMS OF YOUR OWN

THE FOURTH BLOW

The fifth knock
that opened the door
wasn't any louder
than the previous four.

The fourth blow
that split the tree
wasn't any harder
than the previous three.

The third stone
that twinkled like new
wasn't more precious
than the previous two.

The second effort
that got the job done
wasn't any greater
than the previous one.

A poem should smell of erasure.

(I know "smell of erasure" is not modern,
but it is <u>so good</u>.)

POEMS OF YOUR OWN

8) <u>REWRITES AND TWILIGHT...</u>

Then what?

Give your work (draft) time to breathe. Actually, it isn't the one that needs time; you are. When you go back after a day, a week, or even a month, you are in a new mood, you're a slightly different person with new eyes. This is good for your poem.

Let twilight fall between your efforts to rewrite your poem.

> Remember: poems are not born perfect.

REWRITE AND TWILIGHT

Live awhile with your words,
wander along the lines,
stop at the commas,
sleep at the periods, and
leap at the stanzas ends.

Enjoy the twilight, and
take your time. Then,
go back.

POEMS OF YOUR OWN

9) <u>HAND WRITE</u>

Suggestion: write the first draft of your poem by hand.

Why?

>   There is *evidence*
>   that the hand is connected
>   through the head
>   to the heart.

Take advantage of this. I think it's true.

Word processing on your computer is wonderful for editing. Save it for later.

This is just a suggestion. I don't think it a crime if you prefer to write even your first draft on your computer.

POEMS OF YOUR OWN

10) <u>FORM ISSUES</u>

You are going to impose *form* (structure) on your words. Don't let the arrangement of your words be like an unruly teenager.

>Your poem requires structure. Why?

>>Random structure is a distraction.
>>It causes the reader to wonder why.
>>Form provides consistency.
>>Form keeps the poem together.
>>Structure gives comfort.

Structural Concerns: line length, lines per stanza (readability).

Long lines slow the poem and give more rope for the reader to get tied up in. Long lines combined with long stanzas can take on the look of a solid brick of print, heavy, foreboding. Does the reader dare enter the page?

When you set the number of lines in a stanza, and the line breaks between them, you allow the white of the paper to frame your words and make them more inviting. Readers like this.

POEMS OF YOUR OWN

> You are free to be creative
> as long as there's a sense
> of consistency.
> You can break the rules,
> but does it work?

Keep in mind: the reader might lose interest and turn the page.

POEMS OF YOUR OWN

POEMS OF YOUR OWN

WORD, LINE AND STANZA
- ELEMENTS OF POETRY -

The poetic word comes first.
It is concise, special and
sounds right, never random.

The line is a strategic row of words,
a single breath in length that satisfies.
A poem is built line by line.

The stanza is to poetry
as the paragraph is to prose.
It must hold together and break when done.

These elements, done properly, give readers
reason to want more. They direct the readers'
attention, and hold them hostage.

POEMS OF YOUR OWN

11) <u>FEATHERS FOR YOUR DUCK</u>

Put feathers on your duck.

> Use vivid word pictures.
> Make them interesting and unique.
> We humans think in images.
>
> Avoid resembling the back side of a tapestry.
> It is only a dull outline
> with a vague likeness to the front.
>
> Choose your words carefully
> knowing that each word counts.
> Make your duck alive and touchable.

Your poetry, your word selection, must be concise and unambiguous. Anything less will leave your readers unsure with a muddled impression.

> *They will surely jump out of your poem.*

POEMS OF YOUR OWN

12) THE FIVE SENSES

Use the five senses as more feathers. (*sight, sound, smell, taste, touch*) The world you describe in your poem does not exist in a vacuum. The reader needs to see it, touch it, smell it, and when ready, take it in.

- Sight- you want the reader to see what you see; provide details, *the dried blood on his face told me he was in a fight.*

- Sound- few settings are totally silent, describe what can be heard: *birds, a creak, or the laughter of children.*

- Smell- this is the most nostalgic sense that instantly connects you with memory, *pot roast cooking in Mom's kitchen, alcohol on his breath.*

- Taste- use when eating, drinking or *kissing.*

- Touch- painful or pleasurable, *a punch in the nose, or cool cotton sheets.*

*We had gone back and forth all night on the ferry.
It was bare and bright, and smelled like a stable—*
  from Recuerdo by Edna Vincent Millay

POEMS OF YOUR OWN

13) <u>REVEAL</u>

Did you reveal something with your words? The best poems give human insight. Writing personal poetry may feel like you are standing in front of your house in your underwear. Yes, you are exposed. That is an integral part of writing poetry.

Write, inspired by what you know—you, your life.

(Let your poem get you in a little trouble.)

Poetry is writing where:

we remember love and possible loss,
we describe wounds and healing,
we can say goodbye to sadness.

Poets lead a life of shared experiences.

Before I dared kiss a man, I kissed Elizabeth.
Love as If Love by Richard Blanco

Sometimes, leave your compass at home.
after Renoir

Write as though you are already dead.
after Nadine Gordimer

POEMS OF YOUR OWN

COWBOY

I never told you this:
when I was a kid,
I longed to be a cowboy.
I'd be a man with an iron code,

one who respected the old,
and was polite to women,
a hero indifferent to
what others thought of him,

who stood tall and talked straight,
when he talked at all.

In Dallas, back in December,
I bought a handsome western hat
with a black leather band,
kept it on my closet top shelf.

Last night I showed it to you.
You laughed, big belly laughs.
Maybe I should have told you,
I always wanted to be a cowboy.

POEMS OF YOUR OWN

POEMS OF YOUR OWN

14) THE SNAPSHOT AND A CAVEAT

A poem is a snapshot, not a saga.

You are not likely to tell your family's entire history in a single poem. It is hard to be born, grow up, have a career, a family and end by playing with the grandkids, all in one poem.

> Focus.
> Condense.
> Define.

Don't write about your life,
write about one day in your life.
Don't write about one day,
write about a moment in your day,
a meaningful one, shine a light on it.

POEMS OF YOUR OWN

THE FISHING LESSON

The first time my Dad took me fishing
we brought a brown bag full of worms.
He selected a big, fat one for his hook,
a small one for mine. I didn't mind.
He saw I was reluctant to pierce
the worm with my hook. Without a word,
he took them from me. I didn't mind.
I was anxious and pulled the line before
he was done. The hook caught his finger,
blood beaded up. I thought he'd be angry,
but he didn't yell at me. After an hour,
he suggested we leave. I didn't mind.
He hadn't caught any fish.
I only caught his finger.
He didn't mind.

POEMS OF YOUR OWN

15) <u>THE CAVEAT - A KEYHOLE</u>

Your poem can be a keyhole; take a look.

> Through a small opening
> a poem can reveal
> a grand depiction.

A poem can describe the Universe on one page, maybe even one line.

POEMS OF YOUR OWN

REPAIR BY THE SHORE

The sign over his garage door proclaims,
BEACH CHAIRS CAREFULLY REPAIRED.
Each morning he sits in front of his business
on a sturdy one and waits for customers.

A grey neighbor lady yearning for company
brings him an old chair in terrible shape, says,
"You can have it for parts, no charge.
Tell me, what are you doing for dinner?"

Two small boys living with their grandmother
bring him a chair they found at the curb. He offers
them a quarter, but they want more.
He settles and gives them each fifty cents.

It's been six years since his wife,
the woman he thought he could never win, had a
heart attack, lingered and died.
After a year of tears, he had no more.

He decided to start a business. So, he put up his
sign and now sits and waits for people
to come to him who need repair. Mostly,
he collects discarded parts and
the occasional smile.

POEMS OF YOUR OWN

16)   **FIRST LINE**

Your poem's opening line (first line) is the most important line in your poem. It may not be the *first* line you write. The first line should make the reader want to know what comes next.

Opening line:
    an invitation, a grabber
    attractive – like bait on a fishing hook
    says hello, come in
    captures the reader
    is straight forward – free of confusion
    avoids knocking the reader out of the poem

Opening line can be:
    emotional, romantic,
    or mysterious in an enticing way;
    an introduction to your purpose,
    not the weather (cocktail party talk)

        If your first line doesn't come,
        leave space for it and move on.

In short, your poem's first line is a diving board that readers stand on. Do they dive in or back off (turn the page)?

POEMS OF YOUR OWN

POEMS OF YOUR OWN

HALF

An Israeli half-brother, I didn't know I had,
showed up at my father's funeral.

Staring at me he said,
"Where's the casket?"

I volunteered, "There is none.
He wanted to be cremated."

"And you LET HIM?"
His words felt like a punch.

"It was his wish." The blood drained
from my face. He paused, then said,

"I am Aaron, he was my father."
"I am Michael, he was my father, too."

With a half-smile he said, "Then we
are brothers. Why do you look so pale?"

"Forgive my shock.
I didn't know I had a brother."

He retorted, "My mother told me
not to come. She was his secret."

"Wait. Who is your mother?
Where is your mother?"

POEMS OF YOUR OWN

"Ruth. She lives in Israel. Your father,
our father, was there for a summer

years ago. They loved each other.
He left not knowing about me. I don't

want anything from you."
I was silent, didn't know what to say.

Then he said, "Please,
may I have half his ashes?"

POEMS OF YOUR OWN

17) <u>LAST LINE</u>

Only the closing line (last line) of the poem is almost as important as the first. I find it pleasing when the first and last lines connect in some way like an open and close parenthesis. Think of the last line as an echo of the first.

Last line:
>the closer
>conclusion
>clincher, but not too clever
>final thought or image
>has finality

Your first words make a promise. Your last, seal the deal. Your poem is like an envelope. You put your words in the envelope. The front is addressed to the reader in such a way the reader opens the envelope to read what's within. After, the back of the envelope tells the reader thank you and goodbye with a rewarding last line.

POEMS OF YOUR OWN

OUR DAY TOGETHER

We walk in the park
where we first met.

We sit on the porch
watching the world get wet.

We lie quietly in bed
feeling perfectly blessed.

I gently touch your face.
You put your paw on my chest.

POEMS OF YOUR OWN

18) <u>THE TITLE</u>

The title of your poem gives the reader important information that helps with the poem's success. Think of the title as a welcome mat, not a summary.

It's the first words read. Make a good impression.

The Road Not Taken - Robert Frost
Because I Could Not Stop for Death - Emily Dickinson
Howl - Allen Ginsberg
Homage to my Hips - Lucille Clifton

How I Met My Wife - my personal favorite

POEMS OF YOUR OWN

HOW I MET MY WIFE

As an 18-year-old lifeguard
on top of the world,
I sat alone waiting to save others,
but she shyly approached, smiled
and saved me. It was 1968.
Her smooth, tanned skin
played hide-and-seek
with her pale bikini.
From my perch I stared far too long.
She asked me if I liked the Beatles.
Trying to be cool I asked her why.
She replied, "I could never marry anyone
who didn't like the Beatles."
I jumped off my lifeguard's chair,
looked into her innocent eyes and
told her, "Ringo's my favorite."

POEMS OF YOUR OWN

POEMS OF YOUR OWN

19) <u>LIFE IS MESSY</u>

Life is messy and confusing and there is usually a "but".

> You are not writing a Hallmark card.
> A good poem paints a real picture
> about the way life and people really are.
> People and relationships are complicated.
> That's just the way it is.

Your poetry must resonate with the reality of life. Flaws are a part of the human design.

> Ralph was my mentor,
> kind and gentle,
> a model big brother,
> at least when he wasn't
> around Dad.

> *The absence of a flaw*
> *in a poem about humans*
> *is itself a flaw.*
> after Havelock Ellis

POEMS OF YOUR OWN

MY MOTHER'S SMILE

I spent a lifetime
looking for my mother's smile.
I can picture a toddler approaching,
his mother sees him and
her eyes light up, a smile erupts.
It's spontaneous, but
I'm not him and that's
not my mother.

Mine held me lightly on her lap
so I wouldn't crush her ruffled dress.
Other times, my dirty hands and face
were kept at a distance,
so was the rest of me.
It's hard to love yourself
when the part of you called *mother*
loves best from behind a wall.

Her outstretched arms
may not have been
long enough
to cross the open space
between us,
but her smile could have—
had she been willing,
had she been able.

POEMS OF YOUR OWN

Now she's gone and
the distance between us
is even greater, so
I picture in my mind
her smiling at me
with an approving nod.
I know I'm lying to myself,
but it's a good lie.

POEMS OF YOUR OWN

20) <u>WHAT'S IN, WHAT'S OUT</u>

Carefully choose what to include and what to leave out of your poem. Artists call this *composition*. My wife, watercolorist Pat Morgan, taught me this. An artist designs a painting by deciding which components are necessary and which are not needed.

You may be aware of many more details than you should include in your poem. Even if the particulars are true to the story you are telling, it doesn't mean they are good and necessary for your poem's success. Your poem must be truer than the facts.

>Fill your poem with
>the needed details.
>Let them tell the tale.
>As your words dry on the page,
>the page will part like the Red Sea
>revealing your meaning.

POEMS OF YOUR OWN

21) READING SOMEONE ELSE'S POEM

When reading and studying (an activity you should consider making part of your daily routine) someone else's poem:

> Look for your favorite lines.
> Consider the poem's content,
> the poet's technique, and
> together, their effectiveness.
> Take notes, mark up the page.
>
> Content,
> technique,
> effectiveness,
> notes.
>
> *We are social creatures*
> *to the inmost center of our being.*
> *The notion that one can*
> *begin anything at all from scratch,*
> *free from the past,*
> *or unindebted to others,*
> *could not conceivably be*
> *more wrong.*
>   - Karl Popper -
>
>
> Poets are their own tribe.

[63]

POEMS OF YOUR OWN

Creativity is only undetected plagiarism.
- Mark Twain -

Homer taught all poets to be
good liars and thieves.

There are at least two reasons to lie in a poem:

First, you are telling a secret about yourself and wish to disguise it.

Second, you find it necessary to change the facts of the situation for the sake of crafting a better poem.

As Mark Twain suggested, we all borrow words and ideas from those we have read and admired. Our responsibility is to skillfully remix and expand on what we appropriate.

Only Adam, of biblical fame, did not plagiarize.

POEMS OF YOUR OWN

POEMS OF YOUR OWN

(TAKE A BREAK)

I USE TO KNOW IT ALL, BUT NOW

If you're a student of writing,
then write every day, at least a little.
If you're not writing, then be reading.
Everywhere you sit should have
a notebook and a reading book
waiting for your arrival.
As you read other authors,
consider their words,
analyze their techniques,
and evaluate the effectiveness of both.
If it's not a library book or the bible,
underline your favorite lines
and take notes in the margins.
We are all students in a world
filled with teachers quietly
waiting for us to sit down.

POEMS OF YOUR OWN

22) FIGURATIVE LANGUAGE

Use evocative, figurative language to describe the unknown by comparison with the known. This is more poetic than an eclectic string of descriptive adjectives. Think of figurative language as the opposite of literal language. It is indirect and likely to be symbolic.

Simile: uses *like* or *as*:

> He was a lot like his toolbox;
> sturdy—made for hard work.
> > from the obituary of Alfred J. Thibodeau

Metaphor: more demanding, more abstract:

> There are years that are questions,
> and years that are answers.
> > - Zora Neale Hurston -

Poetry depends on figurative language to drive its message home; again, more descriptive feathers for your duck.

POEMS OF YOUR OWN

MORNING LIGHT - MY LIFE

I do not add light to the arriving morning,
or fill the cool air with sweet bird sounds,
or pull the tides to one side like the moon,
I simply groan quietly, not to wake my wife,

and shimmy out of my side of the bed and
head for the toilet and then the kitchen,
where the Cuisinart dutifully did its Maxwell
House task without fuss, or complaint.

My life is filled with small pleasures like my
morning coffee. And persistent pains like my
back barking its age. I am contently caught
in the limitations and rituals of my life.

POEMS OF YOUR OWN

23) <u>GRAMMAR GRABBERS</u>

THE APPOSITIVE

This is not a grammar lesson. Naming parts of speech is not my goal; adding more color to your poetry is. Using smart adjectives and sly adverbs may be your first thought, but they are not your only choices.

Consider using an *appositive;* often forgotten, these affirmative words illustrate the target word (noun or verb) giving it texture and clarity. They provide details; they extend and deepen. They add light.

> Ralph, *my congenial second cousin*, liked to borrow money and gamble.

Adding *ing* or *ed* to a verb can make it a useful appositive.

> Cindy waits *thinking this is a mistake.*

> *Tired and disgusted,* Walt wants to go home.

This construct, used sparingly, is part of the poet's toolkit and allows for more singular descriptions.

POEMS OF YOUR OWN

THE PREPOSITION

Then there is the *preposition* and the corresponding prepositional phrase. Prepositions are a select group of words that connect a phrase to the subject giving information about the target noun or verb.

IN SEVENTH GRADE

Mrs. Minnerly,
my 7th grade teacher
at North Junior High School,
made us memorize
40 or so prepositions.
I'm sure she thought,
with the best of intensions,
this to be good for us.

Some of my favorite prepositions: after, at, between, during, in, near, on, over, with—there are more.

during the storm
after sunset
on the bridge
over the creek

POEMS OF YOUR OWN

Use these devices to provide your poem with
details and feathers for your duck.

According to Ted Kooser,
U.S Poet Laureate,
a poet needs to
shake off generalizations.

Seemingly, all ducks have feathers. You, as poet,
need to be specific and give just the right amount
of color and texture to your duck.

POEMS OF YOUR OWN

24) <u>YOUR *POETIC LICENSE*</u>

You have a poetic license. It gives you the freedom to depart from the facts of a true story, to change perspective, or leave conventional rules of grammar behind in order to make the poem yours.

Personal poetry has the potential to be inspired and unique.

POETIC LICENSE

YOUR NAME HERE

Imagination Takes You
Anywhere
You Want to Go

"...You make me feel <u>like a natural woman</u>..."
    words written by Carol King's
    husband, Gerry Goffin using
    his poetic license.

POEMS OF YOUR OWN

GRASSHOPPERS AND ANTS

Grasshoppers and ants
wearing shirts and pants,
both blessings and rants,
some cans and some can'ts.

Her name was Megs,
he liked her long legs.
After finishing two kegs,
they married and laid eggs.

Blessings and rants,
some cans and some can'ts,
grasshoppers and ants
wearing shirts and pants.

She knew he was a winner,
but she was a sinner.
He was so much thinner,
she ate him for dinner.

It's fate and it's chance,
both blessings and rants,
grasshoppers and ants,
some cans and some can'ts.

POEMS OF YOUR OWN

25) <u>PERSONA</u>

>You may choose to use
>(or hide in)
>a different persona.

persona: who's talking

>gives you options
>gives you a disguise
>gives you a chance
>to use your poetic license

"he/she" hides you in the poem better than "I".

choices: male/female
>young/old
>I/she/he
>human/animal/thing

POEMS OF YOUR OWN

Man is least himself
when he talks in his own person.
Give him a mask
and he will tell you the truth.
- Oscar Wilde -

POEMS OF YOUR OWN

THE DUKE AND MY DAD

"Dad, you're staring."
It was 1978, in a Newark diner.
"That's the Duke!" Dad whispered.
"Who?"

"The booth behind you."
Subtly as I could, I turned.
Seated alone, John Wayne,
holding a mug of black coffee.

Dad was up before I could
say *noooo*. By the time I reacted,
he was shaking the Duke's hand;
both were laughing.

When Dad returned,
His face was different,
like he had seen a saint,
an authentic holy man.

POEMS OF YOUR OWN

Mr. Wayne stood up,
took out his wallet and left a tip,
paid at the register in cash,
turned to my father, winked, and left.

As he walked away,
I asked my father what he had said.
"He told me, 'Ride tall,
and leave a good tip.'"

Both John Wayne and my father
died the following year, but not
before giving me their way to see
the world,

and a code to live by.

POEMS OF YOUR OWN

26) THE SOUND OF YOUR WORDS

Call it verbal music. A poem interrupts the silence. Reading or hearing a poem should be a delicious, auditory experience. Originally, poems were either sung or recited. ♩♫♩♫

Rhyme - a pleasant echo of a similar sound.

A bat and a cat will not share a mat.

Rhythm - beats - read your poem out loud.
Do the lines move forward at a relatively uniform pace? (There are exceptions.)
Does it sound right?

Alliteration - repetition of a syllable sound in successive words.

FLIES AND FLEAS

*Do fleas fly
without saying goodbye,
or do flies flea
depending on their bravery?*

POEMS OF YOUR OWN

Attributes - words will fall on spectrums from:

>   smooth to craggy
>   common to academic
>   precise to ambiguous
>   energetic to flat

Choose words whose sounds add to your art.

POEMS OF YOUR OWN

THE HIGHWAY MAN
by Alfred Noyes

The wind was a torrent of darkness among the gusty trees,
The moon was a ghostly galleon tossed upon cloudy seas,
The road was a ribbon of moonlight over the purple moor,
And the highwayman came riding—
Riding—riding—
The highwayman came riding, up to the old inn door.

Follow Noyes' example
with your own
symphony of syllables,
metaphors, and
stimulation
for the senses.

POEMS OF YOUR OWN

POEMS OF YOUR OWN

27) <u>REPETITION</u>

    Repetition is the
    repeating of words or lines
    to emphasize a sound, or an idea,
    or set a rhythm,
    or show significance,
        pay attention—
        something important
        is being said.

Quoth the Raven, "Nevermore."
repeated 5 times
The Raven by Edgar Allen Poe

In rock 'n' roll you'll find the cohesive effect of a strong backbeat setting a dependable rhythm that holds the song together from beginning to end. *The Boss*, Bruce Springsteen, used this often, but most affectively in *Born In the USA*.

(repetition doing its job)

(repetition doing its job)

(repetition doing its job)

POEMS OF YOUR OWN

DUST

I am only dust trying to be a man.
All I can do is the best I can.

I Am Only Dust trying to be a man.
Sometimes I fought, sometimes I ran.

I Am Only Dust Trying To Be A Man.
When I loved and lost, I loved again.

I AM ONLY DUST TRYING TO BE A MAN.
I asked for help and I was given a hand.

I am only dust trying to be a man.

POEMS OF YOUR OWN

28) <u>TO RHYME OR NOT</u>

>We love rhyme—
>some think
>it's not poetry
>if it doesn't rhyme.
>
>Why do we feel this way?
>
>In the cradle,
>our nursery rhymes—rhymed,
>the music of our youth—rhymed.
>
>Rhyme gives auditory comfort.
>>It provides security.
>
>But,
>the poet must not sacrifice meaning
>for the sake of rhyme.
>And, be careful,
>rhyme can undermine
>the seriousness of a poem.

When you write in prose,
You say what you mean.
When you write in rhyme,
You say what you must.
- Oliver Wendell Homes -

POEMS OF YOUR OWN

DR. SCHMIDDLE-SCHMADDLE
(a poem from my children's collection)

Dr. Schmiddle-Schmaddle
was known far and wide.
His helper, Nurse Murphy,
was always by his side.

For the doctor's patients,
only kids were selected,
he made them feel
both safe and protected.

Dr. Schmiddle-Schmaddle
was sweet, much like honey.
His name made children laugh,
it sounded so funny.

Nurse Murphy liked to smile
and often proclaimed,
with all the doctor's patients,
he never forgot a name.

He looked at their sore throats,
as they made the "ah" sound,
gave them chocolate ice cream,
the best medicine to be found.

POEMS OF YOUR OWN

29) RHYME IS ABOUT SOUND

Rhyme is about sound, the music of words. It's an echo, a repeat of something previously heard, but its own.

It's pleasant to the ear, but a devil to poetic meaning.

A Brief Dictionary of Rhyme

> End Rhyme (end of the line) and Internal Rhyme (within the line).
>
> Perfect Rhyme (standard) – the word begins on its own, but ends with the same sound.
>
> Half Rhyme – almost (perfect), but not quite. The words sound related, but more like 2nd cousins.
>
>> The imperfect knight
>> took off his <u>armor</u>
>> and swore to himself
>> he'd live much <u>calmer</u>.

POEMS OF YOUR OWN

Here is the first stanza of a poem my 6th grade teacher had us memorize. I don't think I'll ever forget it (or her, Miss Wagle).

Study the smoothness and pattern of the rhymes.

>RIDE OF PAUL REVERE (1st stanza)
>by Henry Wadsworth Longfellow
>
>*Listen, my children, and you shall <u>hear</u>*
>*Of the midnight ride of Paul <u>Revere</u>,*
>*On the eighteenth of April, in Seventy-<u>Five</u>:*
>*Hardly a man is now <u>alive</u>*
>*Who remembers that famous day and <u>year</u>?*

POEMS OF YOUR OWN

POEMS OF YOUR OWN

30) THINK EVOLUTION

It's not Darwinian, but a poem will evolve with time and rewrites. Only the fittest words and lines survive this essential process.

After writing your first and second drafts, you are not done. Things have changed. Small changes in you and the words you choose will make the difference between a good poem and a better one.

Revisit your poem once again.

Revisit your title (does it still work).

Revisit your opening and final lines. (They are so important.)

Revisit the heart of your poem, its middle lines. Consider cutting from both ends. (Ironic considering what was said above about opening and final lines.)

Has your poem evolved into something different? Is this good?

Words later in the poem may suggest a better opening line.

Experiment with different choices. Be patient.

POEMS OF YOUR OWN

Be brave—undress your lines; make them naked. Expose them.

> Prune
> Pitch
> Replace
>
> Reorder
> Retitle
> Reface

It's not rocket science, but poets can fly to the stars more easily than astronauts.

POEMS OF YOUR OWN

PRUNING POETRY

Be ruthless
Editing is
A heartless
Task.

Poems live not
By their wits
But by
Their words.

Don't use
Twenty
When eighteen
Will do.

Expel
Extraneous words
Until only—
Heart remains.

POEMS OF YOUR OWN

*My greatest strength is
reckless insensitivity to the possibility of failure.*
- Harold Evans -

*Writing is one of the easiest things:
erasing is one of the hardest.*
- Israel Salanter -

*This morning I took out a comma,
and this afternoon, I put it back again.*
- Oscar Wilde -

Don't stop until you've done 10,000 rewrites.
Sure, I'm exaggerating for effect,
but the spirit is true.

POEMS OF YOUR OWN

31) <u>THE SHORT POEM</u>

Write a short poem, one that would fit on a 3X5 card (okay, you can also use the back). Don't write about the full meal, instead, tell the story of the lumpy mashed potatoes.

Write freely in your first draft, then trim the fat, get to the point. Since you use fewer words and lines, 8-12 lines will do, be selective.

With a shorter poem, less can go wrong and that's okay. Read it out loud and decide, does it say enough to satisfy?

(I love mashed potatoes.)

POEMS OF YOUR OWN

ALLIGATOR SOUP

Problem with alligator soup
is getting him into the pot.
Try tempting him with sweet talk.
Tell him he's such a big shot.

Once he's in the soup kettle
put vegetables all around him.
After an hour, if he's still smiling,
throw him back where you found him.

Then go to the soup aisle
at the market down the street,
get a can of chicken soup
for you and your mom to eat.

(Like *Dr. Schmiddle-Schmaddle*, I wrote *Alligator Soup* for a book of children's poems that I have yet to finish.)

POEMS OF YOUR OWN

POEMS OF YOUR OWN

32) THE RIGHT WORD OR NOTHING

It may seem exacting, but review each of your word choices. Remove or replace weak words.

> *Each poem...has an optimum number of words. Going over or under by even one word weakens the whole.*
>   - Charles Baudelaire -

I know this sounds overly strenuous, but I buy into the essence of it.

   Avoid using lazy language -

      clichés (avoid like the plague)
      SAT words (too academic)
      clutter - unnecessary words -
        unexpected surprise
        future prospects

   Logomachy - (from the Greek) - fighting over words. Make it a good fight.

POEMS OF YOUR OWN

WORDLINGS

Words of poetry are seeds.
They are nuclei.
They are suns.

Sentiments grow out of them.
Experiences whirl around them.
Virgin thoughts fly to them.

They invade the reader's brain,
ferment feelings,
grant understanding.

Poetic words water the garden,
dance in delirious circles,
and melt the soul.

POEMS OF YOUR OWN

33) <u>POETIC WORDS AND PHRASES</u>

Keep an eye open for useful poetic words, phrases, and snippets of dialogue.

Collect them in a notebook:
> fresh phrases
> vivid verbs
> nasty nouns (ones with attitude)
> sweet sounding syllables
>> (word or phrase)

They can be found:
> on television,
> when you read
> newspapers and books,
> during a conversation,
>> (yours or overheard)

If they are new word combinations (new to you), or sound like poetic music, don't let them get lost. Write them down. Take generous notes like a diligent student. It is okay if you use lots of paper. Use both sides if you love trees.

POEMS OF YOUR OWN

My First List Of (arguably) Poetic Words:

    ashtray
    betrayal
    comrades
    decimate
    emulate
    gossamer
    imbue
    inscribe
    lipstick
    moment
    myth
    palace
    plague
    suffering
    savory
    tawny
    umbrella

Collect your own list.

POEMS OF YOUR OWN

34) LIGHT AND SHADOW

The light and the shadow of a poem - the plain meaning and projected meaning. Not all poems work on two levels, but the ones that do (successfully), carry more weight.

>The Plain Meaning - in the light -
>>direct, simple, straight, a poetic report.

>The Projected Meaning - in the shadow -
>>revealing, deeper, symbolic, an insight into the intangible.

>>OUT OF ONE, MANY

>>The United States Congress
>>in 1776 adopted
>>as its credo
>>the Latin motto,
>>*e pluribus unum,*
>>out of many, one.

>>In poetry
>>we rewrite this as,
>>out of one, many,
>>for a single poem
>>can be read many ways,
>>each one true.

>>inspired by Rabbi Johnathan Sacks

POEMS OF YOUR OWN

TERESA ANN

She stirs a bowl of oatmeal and raisins
as she has done a thousand times before,
her early morning ritual.
Her life's been consistently lean and austere.
I need little and I have much.

She has a generous heart
that in her youth she gave away.
He did not give his, but he gave her babies.
They gave her swollen breasts.
She fed her babies with joy.

Now grown, they're thousands of miles away
and she sits with her breakfast
at an oak table her father made.
The raisins are hard, but she knows
they will soon soften in the milk.

POEMS OF YOUR OWN

35) BEFORE YOU WRITE

Know this: the poet's task begins long before sitting down to write a poem.

    Believe - believe there is poetry in you.

    Be bold - be brave; your words have meaning.

    Doubts - misgivings are natural and will pass.

    Love something - your choice - write about it.

    Understand - don't wait for understanding.

Just Write.

Try to be one of those people
on whom nothing is lost.
- Henry James -

Be five again.

POEMS OF YOUR OWN

BEFORE THE WRITING

Pay attention,
note details,
mark movements,
make connections
write it down.

Be interested—
even if not. Talk
to yourself,
write it down.

Breathe,
be still,
be alone.

Let your mind
float on the quiet.

Write it down.

Be still when you have nothing to say.
- D.H. Lawrence -

POEMS OF YOUR OWN

POEMS OF YOUR OWN

36) THE MUSE OF POETRY

The Muse of poetry is a source outside yourself giving inspiration.

Famous muses:

> Homer -   Homer asks the muse, a daughter of Zeus, to sing to him about the man of twists and turns (Ulysses) in the first line of *The Odyssey*.
>
> Beatrice - the object of Dante Alighieri's love included as his guide in the *Divine Comedy*.
>
> Zelda - a Southern belle, wife and inspiration for F. Scott Fitzgerald's Daisy Buchanan, in *The Great Gatsby*.

Your muse may, or may not be a god or a person, but simply an unanticipated inspiration that floats out of the ether into your awareness. Be ready when your muse calls. Write the revelation down when this happens, even if it's the middle of the night; it's so easily lost and the muse *will* move on.

Never fail to listen
to the musings
of your own heart.

POEMS OF YOUR OWN

MADAM P

Poetry,
my mistress and muse,
demanding and flirtatious,
on occasion, adulterous as April.
Box cutter sharp—
with just the cock of her head
she can open me up,
expose my gut and sinew.
No frailty is safe with her,
no secret too sacred to expose.
She revels in the rhythm of my words.
Dances to the sound of their samba.
The click of her approaching steps
makes me anxious and then,
when I least expect her to,
she pleases me.

POEMS OF YOUR OWN

37) <u>THE POET HAS TWO FACES</u>

TWO FACES

The poet is like Janus,
mythical god with two faces,
looking east and west
at the same time.

The poet is bifold—mind and soul.
The first is craftsman, and critic;
the second, unquestioning source
of innocence and zeal.

The mind is a technician
whose self-discipline
will be needed to edit
rewrite after rewrite.

The soul is a seeker of solitude
full of awe and appreciation,
moved from time to time to write
an unconstructed first draft.

The poet balances this duality,
the judge and the guiltless,
getting them to face each other
with only an occasional quarrel.

POEMS OF YOUR OWN

WORKERS

Across
the street,
workers me-
thodically add
strip by strip of
grey shingle to my
neighbor's roof, from
bottom left to top right,
careful not to step off the
ever-present edge, or let
gravity take them down the
incline. No wandering mind
could survive this task. They work
silently without stopping as the sun
tests their resolve. Then one of them,
who had escaped the roof, returns, climbs
the ladder with a paper bag, reaches in and
with Tommy Johns precision, throws each of
them a can of coke. They sit on their work and
drink the cold rejuvenator. Their rest is brief, may-
be a minute. Their sweat dries, and then back to their
labor. They must finish their work before sunset, so
they can go home to their wives, kids and dinner.
Then dream about clouds.

Tomorrow there will be another roof.

POEMS OF YOUR OWN

38) <u>WHEN YOU GET LOST AND YOU WILL</u>

You may stray from your routine of writing poetry. Days, weeks or even months may go by without you recording a single word. Don't be dismayed; this is to be expected. It's all too common. We are not perfectly disciplined, although we get frustrated when our writing is not close to perfect.

I implore you, give yourself a break. Be patient. Be gentle. Take a deep breath and you will return to your words when you are ready.

If you are reading this, you are most likely blessed with a poet's heart. You don't have to be Frost.

All poetry is...making connections.
- Robert Frost -

The hard part of being a poet
is knowing what to do
with the other twenty-three
and a half hours of the day.
- Max Beerbohm -

I'd rather be a poet than the President.

POEMS OF YOUR OWN

FORGIVE ME, BYRON

Life's too short
for convoluted verse.
Let the university boys
write their dissertations
about opaque poetics.
I want my poems to be
like a medium red wine,
desirable, accessible at first sip.
And then, on second taste,
new meanings emerge
without diminishing the sweetness
of the first encounter.
I want my words to linger
on the readers' tongues so
they instinctively swallow,
and desire more.

POEMS OF YOUR OWN

THE POET SETS THE TABLE

Imagine a dining room table;
you cover it with a white cloth.
You position the chairs
opposite each other with precision.
You set out the plates and
forks, knives, and spoons,
the water and wine glasses,
the flower array in the middle.
The guests seat themselves;
all places are filled. You are left
standing outside the dining room
as the guests consume the meal.
All you can do is hope they get it.

POEMS OF YOUR OWN

POEMS OF YOUR OWN

39) <u>CONCLUSION</u>

This is not a textbook.
There are no college credits
or certifications awarded.

Now, write your poem;
polish it over and over.
Let it shine from inside.

Word it so it resonates
in the hearts of your readers.
Then, write another.

POEMS OF YOUR OWN

BIBLIOGRAPHY
for additional reading

Bird by Bird – Some instructions on Writing and Life
- Anne Lamott -

The Poetry Home Repair Manual
- Ted Kooser -

The Poet's Companion
- Kim Addonizio and Dorianne Laux -

The Woman Who Spilled Words All Over Herself
- Rosemary Daniell -

poemcrazy - freeing your life with words
- Susan Goldsmith Woodridge -

POEMS OF YOUR OWN

USEFUL REFERENCES
ones I use

DICTIONARY

Webster's Collegiate Dictionary

New Oxford American Dictionary

THESAURUS

Oxford American Writer's Thesaurus

Webster's New World Dictionary and Thesaurus

RHYMING DICTIONARY

New Comprehensive American Rhyming Dictionary – Sue Young

GRAMMAR

The Elements of Style – Strunk & White

QUOTATIONS

The Harper Book of Quotations

POEMS OF YOUR OWN

POEMS OF YOUR OWN

NEWTON'S LAWS OF POETIC DYNAMICS
where my past and present intersect

1st Law of Poetic Dynamics – a poem must work by its own inertia.

A poem will move or be at rest depending solely on its words.

2nd Law of Poetic Dynamics – rhyme must never be forced.

Meaning must not be sacrificed for the sake of rhyme. If the poet must forfeit the intended meaning of a line to make it rhyme, don't rhyme the poem.

3rd Law of Poetic Dynamics – for every word the poet writes, there is an equal, but opposite rewrite.

Word by word, find the perfect word, then check again.

POEMS OF YOUR OWN

POEMS OF YOUR OWN

POET POINT REVIEW

1) What Is Poetry?
   - *carefully selected words* -

2) Why Personal Poetry?
   - *words make feelings more real* -

3) Not Me
   - *yes, you* -

4) Write Every Day
   - *make it routine* -

5) Words Do All the Work
   - *your reader only knows your words* -

6) The Dreadful First Draft.
   - *getting started* -

7) Rights and Rewrites
   - *tune, fine tune, finer tune* -

8) Rewrites and Twilight
   - *time in between to let it breathe* -

9) Hand Write
   - *heart to head to hand* -

10) Form Issues
    - *looking good* -

POEMS OF YOUR OWN

POEMS OF YOUR OWN

11) Feathers for Your Duck
    - *your poem comes alive* -

12) The Five Senses.
    - *see me* -

13) Reveal
    - *write about what's real* -

14) The Snapshot and the Caveat
    - *pick a moment; write about it* -

15) The Caveat - A Keyhole
    - *a peak at the forest* -

16) First Line
    - *says, "come in"* -

17) Last Line.
    - *says, "goodbye"* -

18) The Title
    - *your poem's marquee* -

19) Life Is Messy.
    - *"however" happens* -

20) What's In, What's Out
    - *composition and design* -

21) Reading Someone Else's Poem
    - *study others* -

POEMS OF YOUR OWN

POEMS OF YOUR OWN

22) Figurative Language
    - *select evocative expressions* -

23) Grammar Grabbers
    - *back to high school English* -

24) Your Poetic License
    - *a poet's passport* -

25) Persona
    - *your disguise* -

26) The Sound of Your Words
    - *I hear music* -

27) Repetition
    - *words worth repeating* -

28) To Rhyme or Not
    - *is the question* -

29) Rhyme Is About Sound
    - *a pleasant experience for the ear* -

30) Think Evolution
    - *prune, pitch, replace* -

31) The Short Poem
    - *a file card poem* -

POEMS OF YOUR OWN

POEMS OF YOUR OWN

32) The Right Words or Nothing
    - *weigh each of your words* -

33) Collect Poetic Words and Phrases
    - *collect them as you would sea glass* -

34) Light and Shadow
    - *more than a first impression* -

35) Before You Write
    - *while you are waiting* -

36) The Muse of Poetry
    - *listen closely, the muse only whispers* -

37) The Poet Has Two Faces
    - *like Janus* -

38) When You Get Lost and You Will
    - *be patient with yourself* -

39) Conclusion
    - *epilogue, now write a poem* -

POEMS OF YOUR OWN

POEMS OF YOUR OWN

ABOUT THE AUTHOR

Richard Morgan has written eight books of poetry, most enlightened by his wife, Pat Morgan's watercolors. His poems describe the excursions of his imagination inspired by sixty years of life as a poet, parent, husband, and teacher. He lives with Pat on a mountainside in western North Carolina spending much of his time writing and rewriting and teaching about writing personal poetry.

He can be reached at rsmorgan18@comcast.net and Amazon.com by searching:
> Richard Morgan Poetry

POEMS OF YOUR OWN

POEMS OF YOUR OWN

The Finale

first poem
from my
first book

I AM SEA GLASS

You ask
who I am:
I tell you—
I am
sea glass,
Noxzema blue,
edges worn smooth,
yet one corner still
jagged despite
erosion,
dangerous,
dark and translucent,
mostly unknowable.
More artifact
than treasure.
Surviving.
Surviving.

We are all sea glass being warn smooth.
Life is sandpaper to our rough edges.
We become translucent with unseen depth.
This is the source of your poetry. Write about it.

POEMS OF YOUR OWN

Printed in Great Britain
by Amazon